GREATEST WARRIORS
KNIGHTS

PETER HEPPLEWHITE

ARCTURUS

This edition first published in 2014 by Arcturus Publishing

Distributed by Black Rabbit Books
P.O. Box 3263
Mankato
Minnesota MN 56002

Edited and designed by: Discovery Books Ltd.

Library of Congress Cataloging-in-Publication Data

Hepplewhite, Peter.
 Knights / Peter Hepplewhite. -- First edition.
    pages cm. -- (Greatest warriors)
 Includes bibliographical references and index.
 Summary:"Provides readers with exciting details, facts, and statistics about medieval knights"--Provided by publisher.
 ISBN 978-1-78212-400-9 (library binding)
 1. Knights and knighthood--Juvenile literature. 2. Civilization, Medieval--Juvenile literature. I. Title.
 CR4513.H47 2014
 909.07--dc23
                    2013005699

Series concept: Joe Harris
Managing editor for Discovery Books: Laura Durman
Editor: Clare Collinson
Picture researcher: Clare Collinson
Designer: Ian Winton

Picture credits:
Alamy: p. 7 (Holmes Garden Photos), p. 11 (Steve Vidler), pp. 18, 24 (AF Archive), p. 20 (Jose Elias/Lusoimages—Events), p. 23 (Pictorial Press Ltd), p. 27 (ZUMA Wire Service), p. 28 (Tim Gainey); Château des Baux de Provence/Culturespaces: pp. 21, 22 (Marc Fasol); Shutterstock Images: title (jeff gynane), p. 4 (Mazzzur), p. 5 (Litvin Leonid), p. 6 (Marcel Jancovic), pp. 8, 10 (Raulin), p. 9 (Sergii Figurnyi), p. 12 (Sergey Kamshylin), p. 13l (Boykov), p. 13r (Lowe R. Llaguno), p. 15 (Litvin Leonid), p. 16 (Stanislaw Tokarski), p. 17 (i4lcocl2), p. 19 (PLRANG), p. 25 (Anne Kitzman), p. 26 (Fer Gregory), p. 29 (William Attard McCarthy); Warwick Castle: p. 14.
Cover images: Shutterstock Images: top and bottom centre (Raulin), background (Carlos Caetano).

Printed in China

SL002666US
Supplier 03, Date 0513, Print Run 2357

CONTENTS

MOUNTED WARRIORS

In medieval times (500–1500 CE), knights were the greatest warriors in Europe. A knight was a heavily armored soldier, who rode into battle on horseback. His job was to fight for his king, queen, or lord in battles for land and power.

LANCE

A knight carried a wooden spear about 9–13 feet (3–4 m) long called a lance. He used it to attack the enemy as he charged into battle. Knights also carried swords and other weapons for fighting in close combat.

HEAVY CAVALRY

Knights were **cavalry**, who rode into battle on strong warhorses. Enemy **infantry** were no match for these powerful mounted warriors.

WEALTHY WARRIORS

Knights were the wealthiest and most powerful soldiers in medieval times. In return for military service, they were given land. This made them rich enough to buy the equipment they needed— horses, armor, and weapons.

FIGHTING ON FOOT

When a knight was knocked from his horse, he would fight on foot. Most medieval fighting was **grueling** and bloody hand-to-hand combat.

FIGHTING TALK

Medieval warfare

Knights often traveled long distances to fight in fierce battles against soldiers in other countries. Knights from Western Europe fought in religious wars called **Crusades** against Muslim soldiers in the Middle East.

SHINING ARMOR

Medieval knights fought many vicious battles, as kings and nobles waged wars to increase their power. To protect themselves from deadly wounds, knights wore the strongest armor they could afford. The richest knights had the best armor of all.

HELMET
Early helmets were dome-shaped and had a strip of metal coming down over the nose. This knight wears a chain mail hood underneath his helmet for added protection.

CHAIN MAIL
Early medieval knights wore **chain mail** armor over a padded tunic. The armor was made by linking as many as 200,000 small iron rings together.

SURCOAT
The surcoat was a cloth tunic worn on top of chain mail armor.

SUITS OF METAL

Chain mail could protect a knight from being slashed with a sword, but it did not give good defense against arrows and spears. From the thirteenth century, knights began to wear even stronger armor, made from solid plates of metal. The plates were joined together to make a protective suit of armor.

BASINET
During the fourteenth century, the basinet became the most popular helmet among knights. The pointed visor at the front could be lifted, allowing the knight to keep cool and see clearly, or lowered to protect the face during battle.

GAUNTLET
Gloves called gauntlets were worn to protect the hands.

SHIELD
The shield was used to protect a knight from the blows from his enemy's weapons. Shields were often painted with an emblem known as a **coat of arms**. These emblems helped identify knights in battle.

FIGHTING TALK

Fit for battle
Knights had to be extremely fit to wear plate armor, since the protective suit could weigh between 55 pounds (25 kg) and 110 pounds (50 kg), depending on the design. Beneath the plates, the knight wore a padded jacket called an arming doublet. The plates were then attached over the doublet, from the feet upward. The metal was riveted together or secured using leather straps.

WEAPONS OF WAR

A knight's lance and sword were his most valuable weapons during battle. Knights had a choice of other savage weapons, such as daggers, axes, and maces, for use in close, hand-to-hand combat.

SWORD
Swords were tough and flexible, made from a mixture of steel and iron. Knights often used the same sword throughout their lives.

HEAVY WEAPONS

Knights carried several weapons, adding at least 11–22 pounds (5–10 kg) to the weight they bore. A flail was a spiked steel ball fixed to a pole by a leather strap or a chain. A francisca was a lightweight throwing ax designed to penetrate armor, while a mace was a heavy club with a knobbed head.

BATTLE-AX

A heavy blow from an ax or war hammer could cause fatal injury. These weapons could also be hurled as missiles.

COMBAT STATS

Broadsword—the most common sword
- **Blade type:** two-edged blade
- **Blade width:** around 1.6-2.4 in. (4-6 cm) wide at the base and narrowing to a point
- **Blade length:** 30-45 in. (75-115 cm)
- **Sword weight:** around 4 lb. (2 kg)

Falchion—cheap rival to the broadsword
- **Blade type:** single-edged, curved
- **Blade width:** around 1.6-2 in. (4-5 cm)
- **Blade length:** around 24 in. (60 cm)
- **Sword weight:** around 2 lb. (1 kg)

THE MEDIEVAL BATTLE HORSE

A knight's warhorse was his most precious and valued possession. When enemies came close, a battle horse was trained to bite and kick on command. On the battlefield, warrior and animal worked together as a team.

WARHORSE
Rich knights rode into battle on highly trained warhorses called destriers. Destriers were very expensive **stallions** with broad backs, powerful muscles, and strong bones.

STIRRUP
Stirrups were important in medieval warfare, because they helped knights keep their balance and stay in their saddles when they hit an enemy with their lance or sword.

CAPARISON
Battle horses often wore padded covers called caparisons. The cloth helped prevent sores caused by rubbing armor.

HORSE PROTECTION

As knights began to wear stronger armor, their horses became targets on the battlefield. Infantry soldiers stabbed at them with long spears, and archers shot at them with arrows. A knight would be left in danger if his horse was killed or injured, so rich knights protected their prized possessions with horse armor called barding.

CHAMFRON

A chamfron protected the horse's entire head, from the ears to the muzzle.

PEYTRAL

A peytral protected the horse's chest. Not all knights could afford expensive barding such as this.

BATTLE REPORT

The Battle of Bannockburn, Scotland, 1314

Mounted English knights usually ruled the battlefield, but they met their match at Bannockburn. The English had a larger army—around 20,000 against 6,000 Scots—and expected an easy victory. But the Scottish had prepared well. The battlefield was narrow, so the English army could not **maneuver** easily. When the knights charged, they hit a maze of traps—hidden pits lined with stakes designed to cripple their horses. Those that rode on faced tightly packed formations of Scottish infantry armed with long spears called pikes. After fierce fighting, the Scots advanced and the English army collapsed. Over 11,000 were killed in the retreat.

TRAINING A KNIGHT

Knights underwent a long, thorough training process to learn the skills they needed for the battlefield. At seven years old, boys began their training as **pages**, before becoming **squires** at 14.

SKILLS FOR KNIGHTHOOD

Not all soldiers could become knights. Most came from rich, noble families. At the age of seven, noble boys were sent to the castle of a neighboring lord to serve as pages. They worked almost as servants—in return, they were given rigorous training. Activities included horseback riding, swimming, and wrestling. Piggyback battles taught balance and basic skills for mounted warfare.

PRACTICE SWORD
Swords used in training were blunt or made of wood for safety, but injuries such as gashes and broken fingers were common.

WEAPONS TRAINING
Pages and squires practiced weapons skills every day until they ached with exhaustion.

ALMOST A KNIGHT

At the age of 14, a squire was assigned to serve a particular knight. He looked after the knight's armor, weapons, and horses. He was also expected to fight alongside his master, race across a battlefield to replace broken weapons, guard prisoners, and—if the worst happened—bury his lord.

TARGET PRACTICE

A **quintain** was used to help a squire learn how to use a lance while riding a horse.

FIGHTING TALK

Quintain

The most important part of a knight's training was learning to fight on horseback. A piece of equipment called the quintain was used for this purpose. It had a spinning arm with a small shield at one end and a heavy weight at the other. The squire had to hit the shield with his lance and dodge the swinging weight before it unseated him.

TOURNAMENTS

When they were not on the battlefield, knights showed off their skills and bravery in fighting festivals called tournaments. In front of large crowds of excited spectators, knights took part in mock battles and bouts of mounted combat called jousts.

THE JOUST

One of the main events in a tournament was the jousting competition. Armed with long lances, knights charged at each other on horseback. The aim was to knock your opponent off his horse. Pairs of knights fought until there was only one overall winner.

SHIELD

The main target during a joust was the opponent's shield. A good strong blow to a shield would be enough to unseat a knight.

TILT

Jousting knights raced down the right-hand side of a long wooden fence, called a tilt. The tilt was introduced to prevent a fallen knight from being trampled by his opponent's horse.

LANCE

Lances used in jousting had blunt ends, but knights still often suffered severe injuries.

MELEES

Melees were the spectacular tournament finale. Teams of up to 40 knights battled on foot or horseback. Sometimes they fought *à plaisance*, meaning "for fun," using blunted weapons. However, in a melee, *à outrance*, meaning "to the limit," deadly weapons were used, and there were hardly any rules.

FIGHTING TALK

Dangerous games

Tournaments were extremely dangerous events for those taking part. Around 10 percent of knights were badly injured during a tournament and some were killed. To reward those prepared to take part, big prize money was offered to the victors. Knights often got to keep or sell the armor and horses of the warriors they defeated, too.

INVASION FORCES

Medieval knights often traveled long distances to fight campaigns in lands far away from their own. Large armies of knights, infantry, and archers were formed to invade and conquer other countries. Armies on the move needed huge quantities of food and other supplies.

ON THE MARCH

Invading armies included foot soldiers as well as knights. Knights could only travel as fast as the infantry and supply wagons traveling with them—about 10–15 miles (16–24 km) a day depending on the weather.

THE FIGHTING SEASON

Traveling armies often obtained their food by **plundering** the land they were passing through. So battles tended to take place between spring and fall when fields were full of crops. An area of up to 60 square miles (155 sq km) around a large invading army would be stripped bare of everything edible—grains, vegetables, animals, and even wild berries.

A HUNGRY ARMY

Well-organized forces had field kitchens like these. Each man needed around 4 pounds (2 kg) of grain or vegetables a day and a horse 35 pounds (15 kg) of hay.

A HEALTHY ARMY

A well-fed army fought better and was more resistant to diseases that came with living in the open for weeks, such as **dysentery**.

COMBAT STATS

Norman invasion

In 1066, William, Duke of Normandy, prepared to invade England. His army's daily supply needs in the month before the invasion on September 28 were huge.

- **Army size:** about 14,000 people and 2,000-3,000 horses
- **Food required for men:** 62,000 pounds (28,000 kg) of wheat for bread
- **Fresh drinking water required for men:** 14,000 gallons (64,000 L)
- **Food required for horses:** 26,000-40,000 pounds (12,000-18,000 kg) of grain, 29,000-44,000 pounds (13,000-20,000 kg) of hay, 9,000-11,000 pounds (4,000-5,000 kg) of straw
- **Fresh water required for horses:** 20-30,000 gallons (91,000-136,000 L)

A knight was the ultimate weapon on a medieval battlefield. An armored warrior on an armored horse, he towered above other soldiers. A ferocious charge by a force of knights was usually enough to break lines of enemy infantry and set them running.

CHARGE!
Knights on horseback thunder across the battlefield toward their enemy.

STOP THAT HORSE

To try to halt the threat of mounted warriors, infantry began to develop special weapons and tactics to stop charges by knights. Caltrops were small twisted strips of iron nails scattered on the ground. They were designed so that one spike always pointed upward to split the hooves of horses and cripple them. Pikes were spears, anything up to 13 feet (4 m) long. Squads of pikemen working together could stop most cavalry charges if they were brave enough not to run as the knights hurtled toward them.

Flying arrows posed a major threat to knights on the battlefield. At a distance of 110 yards (100 m), an archer with a longbow could pin a knight to his horse.

BATTLE REPORT

Archers at Agincourt

At the Battle of Agincourt (1415), the English army led by King Henry V was outnumbered—8,500 English soldiers against over 40,000 French. But Henry had 7,000 longbowmen. They fired a vast cloud of arrows—1,000 a second, over 600,000 in total—and shattered the attack by French knights.

CASTLE STRONGHOLDS

Medieval castles were massive strongholds owned by kings and wealthy lords. They were a mark of wealth and power and were constantly under threat of attack. As well as knights, castle owners employed other soldiers—watchmen and men-at-arms—to protect their homes.

PERSONAL PROTECTION

Knights would often act as bodyguards when the lord left his castle.

DUTY TO FIGHT

In early medieval times, knights lived inside their lords' castles, but they eventually became wealthy men. They received payment, and often land, from their lord and collected booty from battles and prize money from tournaments. Soon they were able to build their own homes, but they were still bound to protect the lord and his castle during a **siege**.

LORD OF THE CASTLE

Wealthy nobles such as lords were allowed to own land and build grand castles in return for supporting the king.

UNDER SIEGE

The easiest way to capture a castle was to starve the **inhabitants** into surrender, but if the fortress was well supplied, it had to be **stormed**. Knights usually led the charge, with the support of foot soldiers and mighty siege weapons.

FIGHTING TALK

Siege engines

During a siege, the attacking army would use massive weapons, known as siege engines, to break through castle walls. The trebuchet was a large machine with a throwing arm 66 feet (20 m) long. It could hurl rocks of up to 310 pounds (140 kg) at and over enemy walls. The mangonel was a **catapult** that could throw a missile up to 1,100 yards (1,000 m). It could be used to throw anything from rotting animal **carcasses** to spread diseases, to pails of burning tar to start fires. The ballista was a giant crossbow that could fire large darts 550 yards (500 m).

PRISONERS AND HOSTAGES

The **Middle Ages** was a violent period of history. Ordinary soldiers were often killed in battle rather than taken prisoner or left to die if wounded. However, knights were respected as elite soldiers and had a good chance of surviving if they were captured.

RESPECT AND RANSOM

Knights had a high level of **esteem** for each other, even if they were enemies on the battlefield. In the heat of battle, a knight might be given the chance to surrender and be escorted to safety by a squire. Captured knights were usually **ransomed**—held **hostage** and sold back to their families. As well as showing respect, this also gave the captors the opportunity to make large sums of money, depending on the value of the prisoner.

CAPTURED
When a knight was captured in battle, his life would often be spared. He would be held as a prisoner, but released in return for ransom money.

A KING'S RANSOM

King Richard I of England was captured in 1192. He was locked up in Triffels Castle in Germany by the **Holy Roman Emperor**, Henry VI.

Henry demanded a huge ransom of 150,000 marks (65,000 pounds of silver)— worth about $3.14 billion today! Richard's mother brought in emergency taxes to raise the money.

FIGHTER KING

King Richard I (played here by Sean Connery in the film *Robin Hood: Prince of Thieves*) was known as Richard the Lionheart because of his reputation as a great and brave warrior.

BATTLE REPORT

Agincourt massacres, 1415

During the Battle of Agincourt, the English took many French prisoners. When a raiding party attacked his supply wagons, King Henry V of England thought French reinforcements had arrived. Urgently, he ordered the prisoners to be killed, in case they joined the fight again. Henry sent 200 archers to do the killing, burning some French knights alive in the houses where they were held.

23

CIVILIZED KNIGHTS

Noble knights were expected be a cut above lowly soldiers. In order to achieve this, knights lived by a code of good behavior called chivalry. This meant they had to be brave warriors, but they were also expected to be courteous and honorable and to protect those weaker than themselves.

A FEAST
A chivalrous knight would be highly educated, well behaved, have witty conversations, and impress lords and ladies alike with tales of **valor** at a feast.

FIGHTING TALK

Hunting
Bravery was part of chivalry, so knights enjoyed the risks they took in hunting. The more dangerous the **quarry** the better, preferably wolves, bears, or wild boar. Hunting was a pastime for nobles only. **Peasants** caught **poaching** could be hung or blinded as punishment.

COURTLY LOVE

By the fourteenth century, knights played a game of manners with ladies called courtly love. Each knight chose a noble lady to whom he dedicated himself. The knight would worship the lady from a distance, winning tournaments in her honor and fighting hard in battle so she would hear of it. To please her, he would dress well and be polite to all. The knight's chosen lady remained beyond reach, like a star in the sky, distant and never touched. The knight could never marry her—in fact, she was often the wife of someone else.

TOKEN OF LOVE

In this tournament re-enactment, the victorious knight gives a rose to his chosen lady as a token of his affection.

In medieval times, myths and legends about heroes were common. Knights often played a starring role in these tales. One of the most well known is that of King Arthur and his Knights of the Round Table.

THE SWORD IN THE STONE

The legends of King Arthur were first written down in the twelfth century but were popular stories long before that. Young Arthur is said to have proven his right to be Britain's king by pulling a magical sword from a stone.

EXCALIBUR

The legendary sword, known as Excalibur, was fixed into the stone by Merlin—an **enchanter** and wise man. Merlin declared that only the true king of Britain would be able to remove the sword.

KNIGHTS OF THE ROUND TABLE

Like all kings, Arthur had a band of faithful knights. According to legend, the knights sat at a round table to show that the king had no favorites and that all the knights were equal. Only the bravest knights could become Knights of the Round Table. They had to swear an oath, promising to follow a strict code of chivalry.

THE GREEN KNIGHT

The Green Knight came to test Arthur's knights and was beheaded in a single blow by Sir Gawain.

FIGHTING TALK

Arthur's superheroes

Sir Lancelot: the best knight but also the lover of Queen Guinevere—King Arthur's wife. Arthur never lost a battle when Lancelot fought alongside him.

Sir Galahad: famous for finding the **Holy Grail** after many dangerous adventures. He was the only knight who could sit in the empty chair at the Round Table known as "Siege Perilous." Any other knight who tried died horribly.

Sir Gawain: "The Maiden's Knight," a great defender of women. His fighting abilities were weak at night, but they were three times better at noon.

A NEW ERA

By the end of the fifteenth century, the great tradition of knighthood was in decline. The introduction of gunpowder had changed the way battles were fought. This signaled the end of the knight's reign as supreme warrior.

RISE OF THE FOOT SOLDIER

In the later Middle Ages, heavily armored cavalry became less important on the battlefield. Knights had little protection against the arrows of foot soldiers armed with longbows, and cavalry charges often proved ineffective against soldiers armed with pikes.

KNIGHTS ON FOOT
In the later Middle Ages, knights often dismounted and fought on foot alongside the infantry.

FIRE POWER

The increased use of cannons and guns meant that common foot soldiers were able to fight each other from a distance. Because of this, knights—the masters of close combat—were no longer essential.

CANNON FIRE

Armed with cannons, armies could easily attack castles without the need for long, expensive sieges.

BATTLE REPORT

Battle of Bamburgh Castle, 1464

A famous battle took place at Bamburgh Castle in 1464 between King Henry VI of England and an army fighting for his rival, Edward VI. The castle had survived several sieges. However, on this occasion, gunpowder proved to be stronger than stone. Henry was forced to flee the castle as the walls crashed down around his army.

GLOSSARY

campaign a military operation in a particular area

carcass the dead body of an animal

catapult a machine for hurling large stones or other missiles

cavalry soldiers on horseback

chain mail a type of armor made from small links of metal

coat of arms the personal symbol of a noble family, usually painted onto a knight's shield or horse decorations

crusade a military expedition made by Christians in medieval times to recover the Holy Land from Muslims

dysentery a disease with symptoms including very bad diarrhea

enchanter a person who uses magic and sorcery to put someone or something under a spell

esteem respect

grueling very demanding and tiring

Holy Grail in Arthurian legend, a sacred cup that was sought by Knights of the Round Table

Holy Roman Emperor the ruler of much of Germany and Austria in medieval times

hostage a person held as security for a condition being met, such as money being paid.

infantry foot soldiers

inhabitant a person who lives in a certain place

invade to enter a country or area in order to occupy it

maneuver in battle, to move soldiers

medieval relating to the Middle Ages, the period between 500 and 1500 CE (or sometimes 1000 and 1500 CE)

Middle Ages the period of history between 500 and 1500 CE (or sometimes 1000 and 1500 CE)

noble a person belonging to the aristocratic class

page a boy in training for knighthood

peasant an ordinary person who worked on the land owned by lords and knights

plunder to steal goods from a place

poach to hunt without permission

ransom money paid for the release of a captive

quarry an animal pursued by a hunter

quintain a post with a spinning arm, a small shield at one end, and a heavy weight at the other

siege a military operation in which enemy forces try to capture a castle, town, or city

squire a young noble serving a knight before becoming a knight himself

stallion a male horse

storm to attack a fortified place

valor bravery

FURTHER INFORMATION

Books

Knight (DK Eyewitness Books) by Christopher Gravett (DK Children, 2007)

Knight (Medieval Lives) by Moira Butterfield (Franklin Watts, 2008)

Knights (Knights and Castles) by Laura Durman (Arcturus, 2013)

Knights and Armor (Medieval Warfare) by Deborah Murrell (World Almanac Library, 2008)

The Medieval Knights by Timothy Love and Louise Park (Marshall Cavendish Children's Books, 2009)

National Geographic Kids Everything Castles: Capture These Facts, Photos, and Fun to Be King of the Castle! by Crispin Boyer (National Geographic Children's Books, 2011)

Web Sites

Arms and Armor: Common Misconceptions and Frequently Asked Questions
www.metmuseum.org/toah/hd/aams/hd_aams.htm/
Information about medieval armor from the Metropolitan Museum of Art in New York.

The History of Knights
www.knight-medieval.com/history-knight-medieval-templars.htm
A site with information about all aspects of medieval knights, including training, weapons, and chivalry. The site also includes information about castles and famous medieval knights in history and legend.

King Arthur and the Knights of the Round Table
www.kingarthursknights.com
A comprehensive site full of information about the Arthurian legend.

Index